Old Somerset P...

by

Catherine Roth...

C000205490

Ac '95

Published by Richard Netherwood Ltd, Fulstone Barn, New Mill, Huddersfield, West Yorkshire
Text © Catherine Rothwell 1991
Printed in Yugoslavia by Gorenjski Tisk P.O.

This 1902 photograph of Bristol, "a county in itself" on the border of Somerset, shows many signs of a busy port : a large masted sailing ship, the premises of Charles W. Price, Nautical Instrument Makers, and Thornleys. The broad roadway had until recently been a wooden swing bridge. This city of great antiquity minted coins for King Canute.

Introduction

To be asked to prepare "Old Somerset Recipes" evoked a feeling of pleasant surprise mingled with gratification as we frequently travel the West Country, yet it seemed a logical follow-on after "Old Devon" and "Old Cornwall". Here indeed was a heaven-sent opportunity to revisit places, renew acquaintances and make new friends. Memories flooded back of a wonderful holiday at Halsway Manor near Crowcombe almost thirty years ago when our children were young. Vivid impressions still emerge : the walled garden at Halsway; the pine trees "wet with sudden gold, looking in their last amazement at the sun"; the swarms of tortoiseshell butterflies encircling the purple buddleia like satellites; the huge stag which suddenly appeared on brackening moorland, pausing for a second, head thrown back, antlers stark against the skyline. Moments later the red coat of the leading huntsman flashed forth, the thin note of his pursuing horn echoing. There were marvellous walks in the Quantocks and up Dunkery Beacon, where on clear days a view of 16 counties can be seen. Mysterious swathes of vapour clothed the countryside in the early mornings, draping ancient, thick hedgerows with their multiple species; we even found wild cherries. Quantoxhead, Stogumber, Bishops Lydeard - the names are instantly recalled. Unforgettable too were the trips to the sea : Blue Anchor Bay with its rock pools, red cliffs and ammonites, where we saw a perfect rainbow springing from the Quantocks to arc the bay. Wells, Glastonbury, Bath, Cheddar, the Mendips and Somerset Levels were reserved for other visits, but collectively we came to view Somerset as a land of promise, a county of rich diversity, and every visit seemed to add to this conviction.

The opportunity to collect recipes was thus a golden one, but how would the natives react? Well, they could not have been more kind and helpful. Not merely recipes came forward, but folklore, country remedies and all sorts of fascinating snippets: the story of the witch, for example, whose funeral was well attended by neighbours, but who, on their return to the village, found the witch (was it Mother Melldrum?) frying bacon and eggs for her breakfast. We heard of the "telling houses", crude huts where once the shepherds met to "tell" their sheep at the end of the pasturing season; and Max Ley's hilarious story of the buried venison. It was customary to bury it in the ground. When it was time for the harvest supper, the boy was told, "Go, get the venison". It then came to light that he had put it in the manure heap. However, the supper went forward and the well-washed, well-roasted venison was declared by the farmers to be "best ever". Exmoor venison marinaded in port wine, cooked with onions, mushrooms, bacon and herbs, and topped with scallop potatoes is indeed a dish fit for a king.

The old terminology in the record books of the ports I found particularly interesting : hogsheads of wine and brandy; kilderkins of ale or porter; dickens of leather or arsenic; bushels of apples or pears; firkins of mustard and bladders of snuff; as were prices of food 200 years ago : "for a guse 2/-; for the candell light 1/6; for the chees 1/6; for onions and apples, for sage 6 pence ...". Smuggling and wrecks added to the interest, food and drink constantly cropping up. The Port Reeve's records at ancient Watchet in October 1746 account for "a rumpe of beef 3/4, a surloyne of beef 4/4, a leg of mutton 2-0".

Somerset cooking, we found, is expressed in hearty meat dishes, staying puddings, casseroles, stews and delicious pies, all relying heavily on local ingredients which are exploited to the full. Cider, cream, fish, apples, venison and lamb are the mainstays. Like the South Downs lamb which gains subtle flavour from grazing on thymey uplands, so lamb raised on Exmoor and fattened on the farming areas at its foot, gains superb flavour. This is also true of the trout found in rivers fed by the peaty streams flowing from Exmoor.

I sincerely hope that the sampling of these recipes will prove as enjoyable as the collecting of them. As time went by I began strongly to suspect that the famous people in the past who discovered Somerset: Wordsworth, Coleridge, Turner and others, at a time when these old recipes would certainly be in use, stayed for the food - and who could blame them?

Catherine Rothwell

The 13th century Dovecote at Dunster still has its revolving ladder, used to reach the nesting boxes. In those days when all cattle could not be kept throughout winter and had to be slaughtered as there was insufficient provender, doves and pigeons were a source of fresh meat reserved for the Lord of the Manor and the Abbot.

English Shortbread

English Shortbread was made in Somerset, this type being distinguished by the use of eggs.

1 lb flour
1/2 lb butter
1/2 lb moist sugar
2 eggs

"Put butter and sugar on a board and cream them together. Add the eggs well beaten and rub in a little at a time, into the flour till all is used up. It takes a good deal of hard kneading. Form the mixture into 2 cakes but do not use a rolling pin. Pinch the edges, prick the centre with a fork and decorate with caraway seeds or citron peel. Slip the cakes on white paper and bake in tins in a moderate oven until golden brown."

Thirty years ago we visited Vellow Pottery to watch the making of and to purchase some lovely, traditional cooking pots. It was a pleasure to discover the kiln still active and the "throwing" continuing. We also came across a Kohlangaz Fire Range made by F. Manly from Skipton, designed to take this beautifully shaped terracotta glazed ovenware. We tried out the following recipe in such a pot, with excellent results. Back at home, it was sole occupant of our electric oven. The recipe also is suitably old, dating from 1898.

Winter Broth

3 lb beef
pepper and salt to taste
10 large leeks

Wash the leeks thoroughly and scald under boiling water. Cut them into pieces about one inch long, the suitable green parts as well as the white. Put the meat and half of the leeks into the pot and simmer for half an hour, adding the remaining leeks and simmering on for 3 hours. Skim carefully and season. It makes 4 quarts of broth and probably was partaken of by family and farmworkers round a deal table. Quantities can be adjusted. It is a basic broth allowing for the addition of pulses and more vegetables. Some of today's packaged herbs and spice mixtures or a simple bouquet garni add more flavour.

Roast Chicken

Flavour was given to the chicken by inserting chopped thyme under the chicken skin before cooking, the herbs being mixed with soft butter to form an easily spread paste. To the chopped parsley could also be added chopped thyme and lemon thyme. Rather than stuff the bird, grandmother used to put inside the cavity half a lemon with a faggot of herbs. Put the bird into a roasting tin. Cover loosely with greaseproof paper and roast in a hot oven 200 C., 400 F., gas mark 6, lowering temperature for the last hour of cooking. Remove the greaseproof paper, baste and allow to brown in the last 20 minutes.

Near the Black Down Hills of Somerset at Blagdon a hearth spirit called Chimbley Charlie lived on the holly beam above the fireplace. On one occasion a dinner party was being prepared for a farmer who had scoffed at Charlie. The table was prepared beforehand, groaning with food and drink, but the guests filed in to find a bare board, tankards hanging up, silver put away. The dinner had to be cancelled!

White Sauce for Vegetables

"Thicken a pint of cream with a little flour, let it boil gently and before serving, add the beaten yolk of one egg."

Caper Sauce

Caper sauce, often served with lamb, was made by adding chopped capers and a little vinegar to the following :

Mix 2 large teaspoons of flour to a smooth paste with a little cold water and stir into it 1/2 pint boiling water. Stir the sauce over the fire until it boils. Take it off the fire, mix with it a piece of butter the size of an egg.

Fritter Batter

This recipe goes back to the 1850s and was used for apples, peach and rhubarb fritters.

"To 2 oz of butter, cut into small pieces, pour on 1/4 pint of boiling water. When the butter has melted pour in 3/4 pint of cold water. With a pinch of salt and 12 oz of flour mix in by degrees, beating well until smooth. Stir in the whites of two eggs, beaten stiffly, and use the batter immediately."

Mincemeat Pasty with Hazelnuts

12 oz plain flour	1/4 teaspoon salt
1 dessertspoon caster sugar	3 oz butter
3 oz lard	2 oz finely chopped hazelnuts
6 tablespoons cold water	

Sift the flour, sugar and salt into a bowl and rub in the butter and lard until the mixture looks like fine breadcrumbs. Add the hazelnuts and mix with the water to form a soft dough. Divide the dough in two. Roll each into a rectangle and sandwich with mincemeat and grated apple. Bake in a hot oven until golden brown. Dust liberally with icing sugar and cut into square portions.

"Zummerzet Fritters"

Somerset fritters are different from any we came across in our travels. The pancake mixture contains currants and the fritters are cooked in the oven like Yorkshire Puddings, but they share the common feature of sugar and lemon when cooked. Nothing is better.

This splendid postcard was written from Burcott House, Wells on August 16th. 1915. It reveals the Market Place with a wealth of detail : The Temperance Hotel; H.J. Jones's Royal Hotel; Davy's shop, and the cannon by the Cross, whilst in the background is the great Cathedral dating from the 12th. century. In the grounds of the nearby fortified and moated Bishop's Palace are the Springs from which the city gets its name.

TEMPERANCE HOTEL.

DAVY BRANCH

ROYAL
H.J.JONES

Market Place, Wells

Roast Gliny

1 plump guinea fowl	bacon rashers (enough to
1/4 pint thick cream	cover bird)
1/2 pint stock	seasoning
1/4 pint dry cider	

The prepared guinea fowl should be stuffed with forcemeat, or a bunch of herbs with half a lemon placed in the cavity. Place in a roasting tin and cover the breast of the bird closely with the rashers of bacon; without these the fowl tends to be dry. Cook for half an hour in a moderate oven. Gently warm together the stock and the cider. Pour over the bird in the roasting tin and cook for another 30 minutes, basting well. Keeping the bird warm, reduce the stock from the tin by fierce boiling in a pan. Remove from stove and add the cream. Gently warm again and it is ready to serve with the carved fowl.

Chicken in Cider

1 chicken about 3 lb weight	4 medium sliced onions
2 chopped baking apples	1 tablespoon chopped sage
1/2 pint cider	1/2 pint white stock
seasoning	

Place the chicken in an oven-proof dish with a scattering of chopped sage on the breast. Add the chopped onions and apples. Add seasoning. Pour over the cider and the white stock. Cook all in a hot oven for 1 1/2 hours.

Stuffing

4 oz sausagemeat	2 chopped, peeled apples
1 tablespoon breadcrumbs	1 tablespoon chopped parsley

Mix all well together. As of old, the recipe recommends placing the stuffing in the bird. I cooked this separately in a buttered loaf tin for 3/4 hour at the same oven temperature and served with the chicken.

Cheese Sauce for Poached Fish

1/2 pint fish stock	1/2 pint milk
2 oz butter	2 oz flour
seasoning	4 tablespoons grated Cheddar cheese

Heat the butter and stir in the flour, allowing it to cook for 2 minutes, then gradually add the stock and milk, stirring all the time to ensure smoothness. Add the cheese and continue the stirring. Put in a very little seasoning and cook on for 6 minutes to ensure flour is cooked or it will not taste nice.

This bronze bowl, photographed in 1902 but in use about 2,080 years ago, was found at the prehistoric lake village near Glastonbury. One wonders what sort of food or other commodity it may have held or what part it played in sustaining civilisation so long ago.

BRONZE BOWL ABOUT 2,000 YEARS OLD, FOUND AT THE PREHISTORIC LAKE VILLAGE, NEAR GLASTONBURY.

CHEDDAR 14510

Watchet Fig Pie

As in Devon and Cornwall, Somerset manages to grow figs out of doors on mellow walls. There is a huge, successful fig tree in the lea of Dunster Castle. Cornwall has an almost unique crinkle-crankle wall, designed for fruit growing. Long ago the monks introduced figs, using them medicinally both internally and externally. Fig gardens, though less numerous than strawberry gardens were popular in Victorian times, and when the figs were ripe, customers could eat as many as they liked. Figgy Sunday or Fig Pie Sunday occurs in a number of regions. My father insisted on a pie filled with figs on that day and I recall distinctly two fig pie dates, the second in November, when summer soft fruits were over and the figs made a nice change from apples.

"Make the pastry by rubbing 8 oz of lard into 16 oz flour and when it resembles breadcrumbs bind carefully with iced water, adding it little by little (about 1 1/2 tablespoons) but do not make the pastry soggy. Keep it cool whilst you prepare the figs, which nowadays will almost certainly be from packets. Wash them, soak for a while the loosely-broken figs in a little brandy, snipping off any stalks. Drain and cut into narrow strips. After rolling out the pastry, arrange the figs in the pie dish, adding a light scattering of sugar, then put on the lid and bake in a moderate oven until the pastry is golden brown." This quantity of pastry will make two medium-sized pies.

Cod Fish Cakes

Good Somerset fish cakes are made with equal amounts of mashed potato and flaked cod :

8 oz cooked cod	8 oz mashed potato
1 tablespoon chopped chives	seasoning
1 beaten egg	1 oz breadcrumbs

Mix the flaked fish with the potato. It should all finally be well mashed up with the chives and seasoning. Shape into fish cakes, using a little flour. Brush with beaten egg and scatter on the breadcrumbs. Fry in corn oil until golden on both sides. They were served with chopped turnips mashed up in cream.

On the last Thursday of October at Hinton St. George children beg candles in the village and place them in hollowed large turnips or mangel-wurzels. The lanterns are carved to represent faces, houses or trees. The children parade with the "punkies" held aloft, singing traditional songs which almost certainly are linked with the Celtic tradition, Samain, the fire rituals of November 1st.

Dominated by the Market Cross where no doubt the famous cheeses were sold, this old photograph of Cheddar shows a marked absence of crowds. William Camden tells us in the 16th. century that Cheddar was "famous for excellent and prodigious great cheeses". It is now also famous for strawberries and early vegetables because of its sheltered position from north winds.

THE HARBOUR, MINEHEAD.

58886. J.V.

Watercress Soup

2 bunches of picked, well-washed watercress	1 Spanish onion well chopped
2 pints home-made chicken stock	1 dessertspoon cornflour
	1 oz butter
	1/4 pint cream

Chop the watercress leaves. Heat the butter and pop in the onion so that it softens, for no more than 5 minutes. Then put in the chopped watercress. Gradually add half of the chicken stock, next the cornflour, stirred into more stock, and allow this to boil, stirring well for two minutes. Put in the remainder of the stock, simmering on for 20 minutes. Before serving, swirl the cream onto individual portions of soup.

It is said that at Hazelbury Plucknett a gentle saint, Wulfric, who loved small animals and lived on nuts, herbs and watercress, once found a squirrel hoarding its winter store of nuts in his drinking cup. Rather than disturb the little creature, Wulfric carved himself another wooden cup. When a wren nested above his bed he moved to a draughty corner so as not to disturb the fledglings.

This is a beautiful 1913 evening study of the harbour at Minehead, considered for hundreds of years to be among the safest on the north coast. One of the oldest Somerset towns, its busiest time was when Irish wool was imported to be woven at Taunton ("dark blue Taunton staple cloth"), but the town suffered when the once prolific herring shoals vanished.

Crab Salad

This salad was served 60 years ago at Ilfracombe where my mother went for several years with a factory party.

1 large crab	1/2 gill mayonnaise
1/2 teaspoon mustard mixed with cream	1 dessertspoon Worcester sauce
salt and cayenne pepper	juice of 1/2 lemon
1 tablespoon cream	2 oz freshly boiled rice
1 tablespoon tarragon vinegar	

Wash the rice and cook it in boiling water with a teaspoon of salt and the vinegar. Strain after 15 minutes, separate grains and allow to cool. Take all the meat from the cooked crab and flake it. Mix together the mustard, mayonnaise and sauce. Add the crab meat, rice, cream and season all well with the salt, cayenne and lemon juice. Take a large lettuce, wash it well and dry the leaves. Place heaps of the crab mixture on the largest leaves. With the tiny tender leaves of lettuce make a pattern to set off the delicate meat and serve in the crab shell.

Keynsham, in the 6th. century was, according to legend, over-run by venomous snakes. When Keyne, daughter of Braglan, a Welsh prince, hoped to receive converts to Christianity here, the Lord of the Manor gave her this infested area to tame. St. Keyne turned the snakes into stone. Fossilised ammonites or prehistoric shellfish abound in the area, which tradition claims are the remains of these reptiles.

Pheasant Soup

1 pheasant	1 bay leaf
3 pints water	seasoning
2 leeks	1/4 pint thick cream
2 sliced carrots	chopped parsley
1 celery heart	2 medium onions chopped
1 teaspoon mixed spice	

Place the prepared pheasant in a stewpot and cover with the cold water. Bring to boil, then reduce heat, simmering steadily for 1 1/4 hours. Add the vegetables, seasoning, bay leaf and spice. Keep the bird well covered with liquid and simmer on for a further hour. Remove the flesh from the bones of the pheasant. Strain the soup. The meat can be liquidised, but we preferred not to do so. Add the cream. Heat up very gently and adjust seasoning. Serve with sippets and watercress on side plates.

Halsway Strawberry Jam

2 lb strawberries or raspberries	3 lb sugar
1/4 lb Somerset honey	juice of 1 large lemon

Wash and mash the fruit and put into the preserving pan, then add the sugar, stirring well. Add honey and blend in, using a wooden spoon. Bring to the boil and sustain a rolling boil for 5 minutes after adding the lemon juice. Continue stirring for a few minutes more then pour into hot, sterilised jars and cover while hot.

Milk Cottage Loaves

1 lb flour	2 oz butter
1 egg	1 teaspoon salt
1/2 pint milk	2 teaspoons baking powder

A 60 year-old recipe, but quick and useful today! Grease a baking sheet and pre-heat oven to 200 C., 400 F., gas mark 6. Sift flour and salt and rub in butter. Add baking powder and mix well. Beat the egg and milk, keeping back a little for glazing. Mix very quickly. There is no need to knead. Cut the dough into 16 pieces, cutting 1/3 off each piece. Shape all the pieces into rounds and moisten the top of the large pieces with a little water. Put the small rounds onto the big, pressing them down centrally with the little finger. Do this as quickly as possible. Brush over with the glaze and get the cottage loaves into the oven on the baking sheet. Fifteen minutes in a hot oven cooks them.

Indracta and Drusa, with a party of pilgrims returning from Rome, were said to have been murdered near Shapwick, Somerset, Saxon brigands thinking that their bulging wallets held gold. In reality the contents were seed corn, a gift for the poor. A miraculous light betrayed the murderers, who were forced to witness the re-interring of their victims at Shepton Mallett.

Stogumber Celery Soup

2 celery hearts	freshly ground black
2 oz butter	peppercorns
2 pints home-made chicken	1 medium sliced onion
stock	1/2 pint cream
2 medium peeled potatoes	chopped chives
	pinch of nutmeg

Wash and chop well the celery hearts. Slice up the potatoes and onion, cooking them very slowly in the heated butter until softened a little. Put in seasoning and spice and mix well. Next add the stock and slowly bring all to the boil, then set to simmer for 3/4 hour. Sieve the soup and add the cream, after which re-heat gently but on no account boil. Serve with the chives floating on top.

As in Devon and Kent, we found that celery soup is a trusty favourite amongst older people "to keep off the rheumatiz".

Legend says that guests assembled at Stogumber Church for the wedding of Elizabeth Sydenham were startled by a flash and a hurtling cannon ball which dropped at the feet of the bride. Not surprisingly, Elizabeth took this as an omen, called off the wedding and later married Sir Francis Drake in 1585.

Baked Ham in Cider

a 4 lb joint lean gammon	1 pint cider
1 Spanish onion	parsley
2 tablespoons brown sugar	3 tablespoons breadcrumbs
with a pinch of nutmeg	1/2 lemon
1 tablespoon brown sugar	

Omitting any seasoning, I did not find it necessary to soak the ham overnight and Jim Watson, master butcher, agreed that in doing so, some flavour is lost. The ham, however, has to be a prime piece. Put in a large pan with cider, onion, sugar and nutmeg and the half lemon, simmering for half an hour. Mix the breadcrumbs and sugar. Take out the ham, let it cool and press the crumbs and sugar (bound with a little water) all over the ham. At this point put the ham in an oven-proof dish to which has been added just less than 1/2 pint of stock from the pan. Bake in a hot oven for 40 minutes and the top will crisp. Larger joints will need longer. Damson pickle is the favoured Somerset dressing with baked ham.

Elderflower Water

"Gather the elderflowers when they are in full bloom, creamy in colour, usually early June. Cram as many as you can into a large, earthenware crock and put boiling water over them, allowing an infusion for a full day. Then strain off the elderflower water and bottle in perfectly clean containers."

An old country remedy used for generations as a soothing face lotion against sunburn. It was also added to washing water, rain water collected in butts and sieved, which in those days, free from chemicals and acid, was wonderfully soft to the skin.

The fortified Bishop's Palace at Wells in 1909 was visited mainly to see the swans on the moat which ring a bell when they are hungry. The original 1850s swan to be taught this trick by a bishop's daughter was stuffed and placed in Wells Museum, but there is evidence that generations of swans before this date could also pull the bell rope to attract attention and amuse visitors.

Casserole of Pork from Taunton

3 lb joint of pork with skin removed
2 sliced, peeled and cored apples
2 sliced leeks (white part only)
1/4 pint stock made from chicken bones

1 oz pork dripping
6 peppercorns
4 bay leaves
1 large sliced Spanish onion
3 oz seedless raisins
1/2 pint cider

Simmer the meat with the peppercorns and bay leaves for 1 hour. In the melted pork dripping gently brown the onion and apple. Place these in a heat-proof casserole, add the prepared vegetables and lastly the piece of pork. Add the cider, stock and raisins. Cook in the oven at a moderate temperature for 2 hours.

The brutality with which Judge Jeffreys meted out punishment to rebels at the Taunton "Bloody Assize" in 1685, when 200 were hanged and 800 transported, has led to stories of his haunting the West Country. Taunton Castle still echoes to the tramp of soldiers and prisoners. Spirits hang as balls of light and phantom horsemen with cloaks flying in the wind flee down the Sedgemoor lanes.

Whortleberry Pie from Dunster

Using a pastry made by rubbing 5 oz margarine into 8 oz flour, line a pie dish and fill with whortleberries, sprinkled with sugar. Make a lid for the pie with the remaining pastry and bake in a hot oven, 200 C., 400 F., gas mark 6 for about half an hour.

Country Farm Sausages or Hog's Pudding

Some of the best recipes for this traditional dish have been handed down over generations by Somerset pork butchers and are well guarded secrets. Here is one of them.

Soak some pig skins in salted water. Mix together 2 lb minced pork, 8 oz breadcrumbs and a sprinkling of mixed herbs (1/2 teaspoon each of sage, thyme and marjoram). Season thoroughly with salt and pepper. Fill the skins with this mixture and tie the ends of each tightly. Boil till cooked. Allow a little space in the skins for expansion.

Hog's Pudding is delicious sliced and eaten cold, fried with bacon, bread or egg, or even put into a pasty.

In the early 19th century 342 coaches left London daily for country places. The Bath Mail Coach ran to such a tight schedule, at some post offices on the way, the mail bag was adroitly passed from an upper window of the post office without the coach having to stop. Only 20 minutes was allowed for refreshment (breakfast or dinner) and passengers were usually so ravenous on arrival at the coaching inns, behaviour was unruly. Indeed, the real test of a gentleman in those days was whether he escorted the ladies from the coach. Famous inns, open 24 hours a day, provided refreshment and rest for passengers and stabling for horses.

Watchet was at one time a simple fishing village with great stretches of rock pools holding prawns, crabs and eels. This is the red-cliffed Watchet that I remember, photographed in the 1920s. Its imposing church dedicated to St. Decuman has 13th and 14th century tiles, probably made at neighbouring Cleeve Abbey.

Brown Trout in Cider

3 trout	tarragon
seasoning	3 oz butter
1 teaspoon chives and	1/4 pint cider

Wash the trout well, slit, clean inside, remove heads and pat dry. Mix the chopped herbs with 2 oz butter. Place this herby butter within the slit trout. Place in an oven-proof dish side by side and add the seasoning and cider. Cover the dish and bake for 25 minutes at 200 C., 400 F., gas mark 6. Remove lid 10 minutes before end. Dot on remainder of butter and allow to brown.

Old English Mead

1 1/2 lb honey	1 gallon water
1/2 lb dried hops	1 oz yeast

Dissolve honey in water, add hops and simmer for 1 hour. When the honey liquid has cooled to lukewarm add the yeast. Cover and leave for 4 days then strain into jars. During fermentation keep the jars topped up. Cork tightly when working has ceased and do not drink for 1 year.

In old Somerset when the reeve, ale-taster, hayward and wellmaster were appointed at the Court Leet, after being sworn in, "they all sat down to a hearty meal of roast goose, followed by hot punch and walnuts". This custom at Watchet has survived into the 1980s.

Potted Hough

I discovered that a hough was a hock, or a leg of beef.

"Place in a saucepan a 3 lb hough which the butcher has broken well and cover entirely with water. Put it on the fire at night, let it nearly boil. Then place it on the hob and let it simmer gently all night, not boil. In the morning, the meat will fall from the bones. Mince the meat. Remove the bones and put meat back into pan. Add a little boiling water, pepper and salt to taste, and after 10 minutes only, pot in dishes or bowls and put it aside to cool and set."

This recipe dates from the days when Christmas turkey was roasted "in front of a good fire ... after the bird has been plucked, singed, cleaned and wiped, skewered and trussed, fasten a sheet of buttered paper on the breast and put it down to a bright fire and be sure to baste it well all the time it is being cooked."

Porlock has literary associations, notably the poet and metaphysician Samuel Taylor Coleridge, but its nearby villages Porlock Weir and West Porlock are all steeped in history. The old coach road to Lynton is famous for the steepness of Porlock Hill. Southey, another poet, loved the Ship Inn, which figures in "Lorna Doone". Porlock men beat off the Danes only to be vanquished by Harold in 1052.

Porlock Weir.

58370.

Meat Fuggan

1 lb flour	4 oz lard
6 oz meat finely cubed and seasoned	salt

Sieve the flour and the salt together and rub in the lard. Mix with water to a dry dough and form into the shape of a large, fat pasty. Make a slit down the centre, open it wide and put in the meat. Close the cut, nipping the sided together, and bake for 40 minutes at 200 C., 400 F., gas mark 6.

Fuggan Pastry is used to make Somerset Oggie, a local delicacy which would no doubt be served at the 15th century half-timbered "George", Norton St. Philip. Before the Battle of Sedgmoor the Duke of Monmouth slept there and was fired at by a Somerset man who hoped to win the £1,000 reward on the Duke's head. The Traveller coach ran everyday except Sundays, through Bristol, Bridgwater, Taunton, Wellington and on to Exeter.

Black Puddings

"Get some fresh ox or pig's blood, salt and strain it. To every gallon of blood mix one pint of sweet milk. Mince finely some suet and toast some oatmeal in a plate before the fire. Put this into the liquid along with plenty of salt and pepper and a large onion, minced. Have ready the skins and almost fill them. Tie up the ends and boil for 2 hours but do not boil the puddings too quickly or the blood will curdle. To prepare the puddings for the table toast them before a good, red fire and serve very hot with mustard and cream."

Syllabub

The county of rich pastures has for centuries enjoyed syllabub. To produce the creamy froth, the farmer's wife milked straight from the cow into the bowl. In Elizabethan days "sack", a mead, was added, but later practice favoured wine, sherry or brandy.

3 oz caster sugar	lemon
2 tablespoons sherry	2 tablespoons brandy
juice and grated rind of 1	10 oz double cream

For at least 3 hours soak the lemon rind in the lemon juice. Add sugar, brandy and sherry, then add all this gradually to the thick cream, mixing thoroughly. Traditionally this was served with sponge fingers or almond macaroons.

Sidbury Manor held its Court Leet and Court Baron on the third Wednesday in November. It elected manorial officers whose responsibilities in medieval times included ale-tasting, bread-weighing and meat-tasting, to ensure that villagers had good milk, ale, bread and meat.

At Wells in 1451 a Well or Conduit House was constructed alongside St. Andrew's Well where a spring of fresh water arose. It was designed to carry drinking water under the Cloister and out into the Market Place of Wells. Another manorial officer was the wellmaster responsible for adequate and clean water supply.

THE *ORIGINAL* BATH MAIL COACH.

The original Bath Mail Coach shown in the engraving was inaugurated by John Palmer, son of a wealthy brewer who dreamed of a whole network of coaches covering the turnpike roads. On Monday August 2nd. 1784 the first set off from Bristol through Bath to London. Within fifty years 12,000 miles of Britain were covered by the amazingly well organised system, which reached the height of efficiency and speed in the early 1820s. Palmer represented Bath in Parliament. He received the freedom of 18 cities which he had helped to make prosperous.

Fruit Punch

4 oranges	1/2 pint cider
1/2 lb fresh raspberries	3 lemons
1 teacup crushed fresh pineapple	6 oz caster sugar
	1 pint spring water

Strain the juice from the oranges and lemons and mix it with the pineapple and cider. Boil the sugar with 1/2 pint of hot water for 10 minutes. Add the fresh raspberries and simmer for 5 minutes, then strain off the syrup. Mix it with the fruit juices and when cold, the spring water. The punch can be hot or iced in a hot summer.

Cut and come again cake, cheese sticks, cider cakes, fruit cake with cider, apple cake, dumplings with cloves were suggestions coming from all sides in the Eastover Shopping Centre at Bridgwater, which would seem to indicate that Somerset's traditional cooking is alive and well. For the first time, in Shaul Bakery we heard of Manchips and Lardies, the former consisting of flaky pastry filled with jam. At Watchet we heard of these again and it would seem that the original recipe was brought over by the Huguenots who settled after fleeing from persecution in Europe. (They also brought their skills of lace making and the handling of cloth: weaving and dyeing.)

It is interesting to learn that Watchet became well known for "Celebrated Watchet Biscuits", enjoyed by both sailors and visitors. These were a superior kind of ship's biscuit, much better than "the usual hard tack". The flour for Watchet and Bridgwater Manchips was supplied locally by Messrs. Stoate. Fatcakes and Manchips were consumed in large quantities on "Caturn's Night". A lady, Catherine, either saint or queen, once provided a feast of hot cakes and scrumpy or farmhouse cider, which became a traditional event.

The fatcakes or lardies stuffed with currants resemble Cornwall's "heavy cakes".

Cheddar Cheese Dumplings

2 oz finely grated Cheddar cheese	small pinch of marjoram seasoning
4 oz flour	1/2 teaspoon baking powder
2 oz shredded suet	a little water

Mix the dry ingredients together and mix with the water to produce a soft but not over-wet dough. Shape into little balls with floured hands. Tossed into soup in the last half hour of cooking. these "dough boys" are sustaining on cold winter days.

Almost the same recipe was given under the heading Cheddar Dough Boys when we met ladies in Dunster. 4 oz flour, 2 oz suet and 1 oz Cheddar cheese being suggested ingredients.

I remember the wonderful air at Weston and the brilliant sunshine on a holiday 35 years ago, with the long line of the Mendips and the distant Quantocks, Steep Holme and Worlbury Hill. Fragments of grain have been found in an ancient camp (300 B.C.) near Weston-Super-Mare. There are many lovely walks in the area.

The Square at Minehead around the turn of the century reveals only horse-drawn vehicles and bicycles. Protected by pine-covered North Hill from cold winter winds, it has six miles of sands parallel with the Brendon Hills. Minehead, like Padstow, is famous as the home of the Hobby Horse, the ancient May Day custom going back to pagan times. The "hoss", which dances round town, is accompanied by two men, one playing an accordion, the other banging a drum.

Loganberry Sponge

1 lb loganberries	1 sponge sandwich
1/2 lb icing sugar	white of 1 egg
2 tablespoons thick cream	

Put half the loganberries in a jar and stand this in boiling water over a moderate heat to get the juice flowing. Drain off the juice and allow it to cool. Mix 2 tablespoons of the juice with 4 oz of the icing sugar. With the well-whipped cream spread this in the middle of the sandwich cake. Whip the remaining icing sugar with the white of egg and spread this on top of the cake, decorating with whole loganberries.

How to Make the Sponge

4 oz flour	4 oz butter
4 oz caster sugar	2 eggs

You need very fresh eggs and dry, sifted flour. Beat the sugar and butter to a very soft cream. Sift the flour. Beat the eggs for 10 minutes. Stir them into the creamed butter and mix very well. Add the flour a little at a time, beating constantly. Turn the sponge mixture, which should look rather like batter, into 2 floured sandwich tins and bake in a moderate oven for 40 minutes.

Somerset Oggie

These are made with fuggan pastry i.e.

1 lb flour	4 oz lard
1 teaspoon salt	

The pig fat is rubbed into the flour and salt and the pastry made by adding a little water and rolling out. Fuggan makes a large pasty. Roll out 2 rounds. Fill with 10 oz chopped pork, 2 oz chopped bacon, 1 teaspoon sage, and use a beaten egg to bind. Put a lid on the pasty after moistening edges, then seal well, pressing together the 2 rounds. Brush top with a little egg and bake in a moderate oven for 3/4 hour.

Greengage Fool

1 lb ripe greengages	1 gill cream
1/4 lb pounded sugar	2 tablespoons water

Put the cleaned greengages in a pan with the sugar and 2 tablespoons of water and stew gently. Rub this through a sieve. Crack 4 of the greengage kernels. Blanch and chop these up finely. Add to the greengage puree. Whip the cream until stiff and mix with the puree. Fill a bowl or individual glasses and allow to set. Serve with cream or custard.

Apricots could be used instead. This apricot filling is excellent as sandwich in a butter sponge cake:

Combine 1 cup of thick apricot sauce made by stewing sweetened, strained apricots flavoured with a little brandy and 1 cup of clotted cream, whipped.

Bilberry Pie

Shervage Wood was once famous for bilberries but a shepherd and two gypsies vanished whilst they were picking the berries and the legend of the Great Worm arose. One Crowcombe lady who made a living out of the pies could find no one to pick the bilberries until a woodman from Stogumber arrived. Seated on a log, drinking cider and eating cheese, the woodman suddenly felt the log writhe beneath him. Quick as a flash he chopped off both ends. One end slithered off to Kingston St. Mary and the other to Bilbrook near Minehead and that was the end of the Worm. Meanwhile the woodman delivered a great hatful of bilberries to be made into pies.

"Make the pastry by rubbing 4 oz lard into 8 oz flour until it resembles breadcrumbs. Bind with 1/2 gill of water. Use only tips of fingers and keep everything cool. Roll out the pastry. Line a deep pie dish and put in a generous pound of washed bilberries. Make a lid for the pie. Gently press down to cover fruit, which should have had moist sugar added according to taste. Cook in a hot oven for half an hour."

Chocolate Fudge

3 cups sugar	1 cup cream
2 oz unsweetened chocolate	1 tablespoon butter

Put sugar, cream and chocolate into a pan. Stir and boil until it makes a soft ball when tested in water. Take from the fire. Add the butter. Cool and stir until creamy. Pour onto buttered plates and cut into squares.

This photograph of Old Cleeve taken by H.H. Hole of Williton in the 1900s shows a typical Somerset whitewashed, thatched dwelling with roses, honeysuckle and lavender in the garden. Cleeve Abbey was known to be in "the Flowery Vale". Old Cleeve, half way between Washford and Blue Anchor, has a far-famed shrine in its Lady Chapel.

Roast Beef with Gherkins and Suet Pudding

More than 1,300 years ago the farmers used to fatten their cattle in such rich pastures, these were know in Saxon times as the Summer Land. It has come down to us as Somerset.

The Baron of beef was equivalent to the "Saddle" in lamb and consisted of a double sirloin. To make it tender the beef was well hung then put in a large baking tin in a hot oven. After 15 minutes the heat was reduced and the meat basted regularly every quarter of an hour. This was considered very important. One quarter of an hour cooking time was allowed for each pound, plus an additional quarter. In older kitchens a meat jack would be used to suspend the meat for the roasting. The rich sediment of gravy was always served with the beef. The fat was poured into a pan in which slices of plain suet roll were browned, ready to serve round the meat.

The Sauce

Put the yolk of an egg in a basin with a quarter of a teaspoon of mustard mixed with a little cream. Add, drop by drop, enough salad oil to form a thick paste. Stir in a tablespoon of finely chopped gherkins.

Easter Cake

1/2 lb flour	1/2 oz yeast
1 teaspoon caster sugar	1 gill lukewarm water
8 oz currants	4 oz raisins
4 oz candied peel shredded	1 teaspoon mixed spice
2 eggs	4 oz butter
2 oz sugar	1 teaspoon salt

Sieve flour and salt into a basin and make a hollow in the centre. Beat the yeast and a teaspoon of sugar to a cream in another basin and add the lukewarm water. Pour into the hollow in the flour. Work in the flour gradually to a smooth dough. Cover and leave for one hour in a warm place to rise.

Beat the butter and sugar to a cream and add the eggs one by one, beating well. When the dough has risen add the creamed butter and eggs, working well in until smooth. Stir in the fruit spice and peel. Leave to rise again for another hour in a warm place, then put the mixture in a greased tin lined with 2 thicknesses of greased paper. Place the tin on a baking sheet and cook the cake for 2 hours in a moderate oven. When cold, cover the cake all over with almond paste. Put a roll of paste round the top and place in a moderate oven for 10 minutes to brown the almond paste very lightly.

Stuffing for Christmas Goose or Turkey

"Crumb 2 slices of bread, beat in 2 oz butter, finely chopped parsley, pinch of salt. Drop in 2 eggs without beating and mix all thoroughly together. A little nutmeg gives a pleasant taste."

Braised Chard Lamb

2 lb loin of lamb	forcemeat
1/2 lemon	1 oz butter
1 large Spanish onion	blade of mace
1 dessertspoon thyme and	1 gill cream
rosemary mixed	1 teaspoon arrowroot
2 rashers bacon	

Bone the lamb and skin downwards. Cover with forcemeat, roll up and secure with butchers' skewers. Put the bones in a saucepan with the peeled, chopped onion, the thyme and rosemary and 2 slices of lemon, peeled and pithless. Add 1/2 pint of water. Rub the lamb with a piece of cut lemon and spread the rashers of bacon on it. Place the lamb on the bones in the pan, cover well and cook gently for 2 hours with the blade of mace.

Take out the lamb and keep it hot. Strain the liquid into a bowl after skimming, boil it quickly to reduce in volume. Mix the arrowroot with a little cold water, stir it into the pan and continue stirring until it has boiled for 5 minutes. Put in the butter and cream but do not allow to boil. This rich sauce is poured over the lamb and vegetables to serve as garnish are placed around the joint.

Sweet Tomato Chutney

6 lb green tomatoes	2 lb onions
2 tablespoons salt	2 lb brown sugar
8 peppercorns	1/2 oz chillies
a piece of root ginger	enough malt vinegar to cover

Remove stalks from tomatoes and wipe them clean with a cloth. Cut into quarters. Peel and slice the onions and bruise the ginger. Place the ginger and peppercorns in a muslin bag. Chop the chillies. Into a deep dish arrange the sliced tomatoes and onions. Sprinkle with salt and mix the chillies with them. Leave until next day, then drain off the liquid. Put the tomatoes, onions and chillies into an enamel pan with the spices and sugar. Cover with vinegar and bring to the boil, then simmer until brown. Remove the bag of spices and pot the chutney in warm, dry jars. Cover when cold.

Fruit Gingerbreads from Minehead

1/2 lb flour	1 oz blanched, sliced almonds
1 tablespoon demerara sugar	1/4 lb golden syrup
3 oz butter	3 teaspoons ground ginger
1/2 teaspoon bicarbonate of soda	1 egg
	3 tablespoons milk
1 oz sliced peel	2 oz stoned raisins

Put sugar, butter and syrup in a pan and dissolve over low heat. Take off fire. Mix the ground ginger with the flour and stir into the syrup mixture. Add the egg well beaten and the milk with the soda dissolved in it, the almonds, the raisins and the peel. Beat well and turn without delay into well greased tins. Bake for 45 minutes in a moderate oven. Allow to cool then cut into squares.

Sally Lunn

1 lb flour	2 oz butter
1 egg	1 oz sugar
pinch of salt	1 oz yeast
1 teaspoon caster sugar	1/2 pint lukewarm milk

Mix the sugar and the salt with the flour. Rub in the butter. With the caster sugar, cream the yeast, adding a tablespoon of milk. Allow to stand in a warm place for 10 minutes then add it to the well in the flour. Mix in half the flour then put in the beaten egg and mix to a soft dough with the milk.

Grease 8 large patty tins. Knead the dough very well and place portions of it in the tins but only half fill. Leave them in a warm place till doubled in size. Bake in a hot oven for 20 minutes.

The Sally Lunns my sister and I had in Bath over forty years ago were richer in ingredients than those of this recipe although it was wartime. The sad-looking Pump Room was closed and there had been a direct hit by enemy action on the centre of the Royal Crescent. These golden yeasty cakes are still made in Bath, the name deriving from the old French, a corruption of soleil (sun) and lune (moon), which well describes them.

Dunster Church, formerly part of the priory and shown in this photograph from the turn of the century, has the longest rood screen in England. The Luttrell Psalter, prepared in the 14th century at the Great Castle on the hill is a chief source of information about medieval life; food, costumes, customs, all appear in drawings. The broad main street with its famous Yarn Market, the road leading to Dunster Church, and the picturesque packhorse bridge across the River Avill make up a lively Somerset village.

Dunster Church.

Buttermilk Scones

2 large cups flour
1 1/2 teaspoons baking powder
buttermilk

1 tablespoon caster sugar
2 large eggs

Mix the sugar, baking powder and flour together, add the beaten eggs and about 1 1/2 cups of buttermilk to make a thin, smooth, lump-free batter. Drop the batter, a little at a time, on a greased, hot girdle and cook for 5 minutes, turning the scones to cook the other side. These are scones to be eaten fresh with butter.

Damson Pickle

3 lb damsons
1 teaspoon cloves encased in muslin

2 lb sugar
3/4 pint cider vinegar

Stone the fruit (quite the hardest part) and pour the cider vinegar over the damsons. Leave them for 14 hours, then next day strain off the juice, boil it up and pour once more over the fruit. Repeat this process add sugar then boil all up together for 1/2 hour. Remove the cloves in muslin and put the pickled damsons in clean, warm jars.

Golden Plum Charlotte

Butter a shallow pie dish and line with slices of bread and butter. Sprinkle with brown sugar. Halve the one lb of golden plums and pack cut side up in dish, adding 2 oz sugar to the layers. Cover with bread and butter (butter side uppermost). Bake until the plums are cooked, then turn out and serve with clotted cream.

Crab with Anchovy

the meat of 2 medium-sized crabs
3 anchovy fillets
3 tablespoons wholemeal breadcrumbs

1/4 pint fish stock
pinch of basil
pepper and salt
2 oz butter

Pound up the anchovies in a bowl. Add the breadcrumbs, stock and basil and bring to boil. Simmer for 4 minutes. Mix the crab with the butter and add to the warmed anchovies etc. Cook for 5 minutes, stirring well, and serve in scallop shells with buttered wholemeal toast.

Blackberry Cobbler from Weston-Super-Mare

1 lb blackberries
6 oz flour

4 oz sugar
4 oz butter

Place the washed, juicy blackberries in a greased dish with 2 oz sugar scattered amongst the fruit. Dot with a little butter. Rub the butter into the flour and stir in the remaining sugar. Knead a little and press gently onto the top of the fruit. Bake in a hot oven for 35 minutes. Serve with cream.

Oare Church and Badgworthy Water cannot be omitted. Here Lorna Doone, immortalised by R.D. Blackmore's moving story of Exmoor, was shot at the altar as she was about to marry the strapping John Ridd. Tom Faggus the highwayman and the dangerous bog on the moorlands called The Chains, near Simonsbath, also come to mind from "a simple tale told simply, of the parish of Oare in Somerset". In Taunton brook, John Ridd "plucked the very best cresses that ever man put salt on".

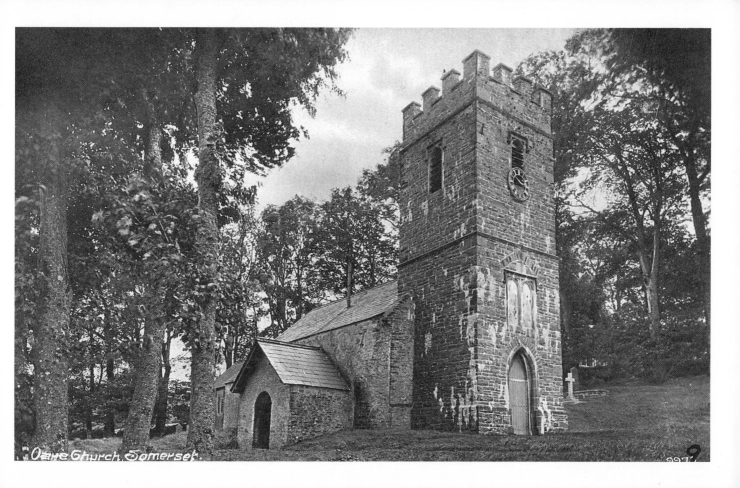

Oare Church, Somerset.

997

Beastings

Harvest home suppers were occasions of rejoicing, involving a good spread of country food, songs sung, toasts to the master and mistress, then dancing to the fiddle. Reading about the faggers' or farmworkers' supper which preceded harvest home and was prepared for gangs of itinerant farmworkers, it seems that meat and herb pasties, boiled hams, roasted fowls, bowls of baked potatoes washed down with beer and cider were set on the table at 7 o'clock in the evening. At 9 o'clock "we did give them more to eat and filled up their mugges and did pay them for their work, and did give each a handful of baccy."

Two days later followed the real harvest home: "6 bigge fowels, 3 hares, 2 gret bigge hams and a bakon chine ... tartes, custards and other swete things." Drinks consisted of beer, cider, brandy, wines, "with milk and lemmon water for the youngsters."

If a cow had calved, beastings were available to make rich puddings. Only of interest today as a recipe from long ago, the "beastinges" were strained, sugar, muscatel raisins and currants added, cinnamon dusted on top, then they were baked "for nearly two howers by the clocke." It must have been a very slow oven to prevent curdling.

The Cider Sauce

Simmer 1 pint of cider and 4 oz sugar until the volume is much reduced, then add 1 oz unsalted butter. Pour over the apple pudding.

Boiled Fruit Cake
(which I understand is traditional)

This boiled fruit cake was suggested by a lady in Porlock although quantities have resulted from my own baking. The idea of boiling a cake was quite new to me.

12 oz raisins	3 oz shredded candied peel
6 oz demerara sugar	1/2 pint milk
2 oz flaked almonds	4 oz butter
1/2 teaspoon mixed spice	2 eggs
12 oz flour	1/4 teaspoon bicarbonate of soda

Place all in a saucepan except the eggs and flour. Bring to the boil and simmer for 6 minutes. Cool. Stir in the eggs and flour. Line a cake tin with treble thickness of greaseproof paper. Pour mixture into tin and bake at 170 C. for 2 hours, lowering temperature a little towards the end of baking.

The Suet Crust

3 oz plain flour	1 teaspoon baking powder
3 oz shredded suet	

Mix all well together and bind with a little water, enough to make a firm paste. Use at once. One hundred years ago some cooks used beef marrow instead of suet.

The Boiled Egg Custard for Somerset Pudding

1 pint milk   3 eggs
1 oz sugar

Beat the eggs and boil the milk. Add it gradually to the strained, beaten eggs. Stir in the sugar. Using a double boiler or standing the custard in a jug in a pan of hot water, stir over gentle heat until the custard is thick and smooth.

Oat Cakes

1/2 lb medium oatmeal   1 oz fine oatmeal
2 oz butter   1/2 pint boiling water
1/2 teaspoon salt

Mix salt with oatmeal. Melt the butter and put it in a cup. Fill up with the boiling water. Pour this into the oatmeal and beat it very well to get air into the mixture. When it has cooled, knead it into a dough. Sprinkle fine oatmeal onto a baking board and roll out this dough very thinly. Cook on a moderately hot griddle until crisp. The dough can be cut into convenient shapes or rolled out into large ovals.

Venison Stew

"Cut the venison meat in pieces as for stewing and brown all the pieces in butter. Add half an ounce each of black pepper, ground cloves, ground cinnamon and ground nutmeg. Mix all well together and put in a pint of good meat stock. Cover very well and cook in a slow oven until the venison is tender. About three hours brings out the flavour of spiced meat."

A Potpourri of Sweet Herbs

could be prepared by drying or hanging in separate bunches :

rosemary, bergamot, mint, thyme, bay, verbena, scented geranium.

Layered in jars, these were sprinkled with bay salt, ground cloves and cinnamon, lavender flowers and dried, ground tangerine peel. It was stuffed into cushions and left around in bowls.
 Somerset grows wonderful lavender. An old recipe for :

Lavender Sugar

Clean and dry sprigs of lavender. Place in a screw-topped jar and fill up with caster sugar. Shake well. Leave for a week, shaking daily. The flavoured sugar was used in junkets or milk drinks.

Parsley Honey

Parsley honey was recommended for the nerves.

 Place freshly picked, washed parsley in a pan (half fill it). Boil for 1/2 hour with 1/4 pint of soft water and the rind of 1 lemon. Strain and to every pint of juice produced, add the juice of 2 lemons and 1 lb of sugar. Boil quickly until it thickens into a syrup. Pot as you do jam. The parsley honey was eaten as a sweetmeat on bread and butter or with cold meats, like mint jelly.

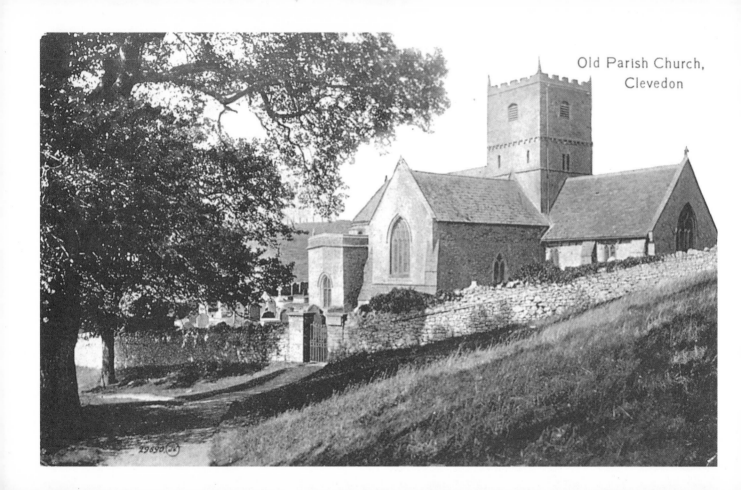

Old Parish Church, Clevedon

29690.

Wild Rabbit in Cider

"Joint the washed rabbit and cover the joints in seasoned flour. In 2 oz butter shake some finely chopped onions and 1 chopped celery heart. Place in a casserole then brown the joints of rabbit in the butter, adding more butter if needs be. Place in the casserole, with seasoning, 1/2 pint cider and a bunch of herbs. Cook for half an hour in a moderate oven. Take out and stir; add 1/4 pint of cream. Put the lid back on the casserole and continue cooking until rabbit is tender, about 2 hours."

Cider is well known in the West Country as a marinade. Cheaper cuts of beef marinated overnight in cider become tender in the cooking as cider breaks down the meat fibres.

This dish was eaten on Plough Monday, the Monday following the Feast of Epiphany, when the village plough was taken into the church and blessed before the altar. "Collops" of beef were eaten on Collop Monday. The aches and pains of ploughmen and other outdoor workers were eased by rubbing on neatsfoot oil. We noted down some old Somerset remedies, one being: "To soothe a burned mouth chew a clean comfrey leaf".

The 11th century Parish Church at Clevedon, looking seaward, dominates the whole town. Here are buried Arthur and Henry Hallam, the former, a friend of Alfred Lord Tennyson, who was the poet's inspiration for "In Memoriam". Clevedon Court nearby is a manor house also with literary associations. Both Tennyson and Thackeray stayed there as guests of the Elton family.

Brown Betty

1 lb cooking apples	3 tablespoons syrup
4 oz brown breadcrumbs	rind and juice of 1 lemon
2 oz demerara sugar	1 teaspoon allspice

Wash, peel and core the apples. Slice them very finely. Put a layer in the pie dish, cover with breadcrumbs and sprinkle with sugar and spice. Repeat these layers. When the dish is full add lemon juice, syrup and scatter the grated lemon rind. Bake in a moderate oven for 30 minutes. This too was served with lots of thick cream.

Kali

1/2 lb ground white sugar	1/4 lb tartaric acid
1/4 lb bicarbonate of soda	40 drops of lemon essence

Add the essence to the sugar then the other powders (all the powders should be dry). Stir altogether and pass twice through a hair sieve, so that they are well mixed.

Must be kept in tightly corked bottles and only a dry spoon inserted. A large teaspoon dissolved in a two thirds full tumbler of water made a refreshing if acidic drink, which was much appreciated 80 years ago along with nettle beer, herb beer, broom wine and ginger ale, all of which could be produced cheaply.

Cider Sauce

2 lemons 1/4 pint cider
1/4 pint water 8 oz sugar

Grate the rind from 2 lemons then squeeze the juice out. Place into a saucepan with sugar, cider and water. Mix well and simmer for 1/4 hour until the mixture becomes syrupy.

This is a good old Somerset sauce for steamed puddings such as

Honey Pudding.

It is still the custom at the Luttrell Arms, Dunster, to burn a faggot or bundle of 12 ash branches in the great fireplace. This has been done since medieval times. As each ash band binding the faggot burns through, another round of hot punch is ordered from the bar. As the wood burns, the Dunster Carol is sung. When the last bit is consumed, a fragment is taken out to light next year's fire. Burning the Ashen Faggot was once a widespread Somerset custom on Christmas Eve.

In 1930 threshing was done in this fashion all over the country, mechanisation being introduced in the 19th century, but in Somerset the ritual of "opening the harvest" survived for many years. Led by the parson, Parish Bible in hand, sickle strapped to his back, farmers, farmers' wives, milkmaids, labourers and children followed. Parson cut the first three swaths, following prayers and a psalm, then the whole party commenced cutting the corn, gathering it into sheaves and stooking it. The farmer whose turn it was to "open", came immediately behind the cleric, bearing a loaf of his own bread and a keg of cider on his back.

Somerset Pudding

2 lb cooking apples grated rind of 1 lemon
pinch of cinnamon 6 oz sponge cake
3 oz caster sugar 2 oz icing sugar
1 pint egg custard white of 1 egg

Peel, core and cut up apples and place in a stewpan with the caster sugar, cinnamon and grated lemon rind. With a small amount of water stew gently until the apples fall. Crumble the sponge cake, then arrange alternate layers of apple and cake crumbs. Pour over this the egg custard. Whip the egg whites stiffly and pile on top. Brown in a slow oven for 5 minutes.

Farmhouse Cake from Porlock

Sometimes called "Heavy Cake" in the West Country.

3/4 lb flour 2 oz caster sugar
1 oz butter 1 oz lard
2 oz raisins 2 oz currants
pinch of cinnamon and 1 egg
nutmeg 1 tablespoon milk
1/2 teaspoon mixed spice 1 oz candied peel
pinch of salt

Mix salt with flour and rub in the fats. Add spices, sugar, currants, raisins and sliced candied peel. Mix well. Add the well beaten egg and milk to produce a rather stiff dough. Roll out this dough into a flat, round cake 2 inches thick. Place in a greased baking tin and bake in a moderate oven for 1/2 hour.

Gruel

| 1 oz fine oatmeal | 1/2 pint milk |
| 1/2 pint water | pinch of salt and sugar to taste |

Mix the oatmeal to a thin paste with a little water, putting the milk in a saucepan with the remainder of the water and bringing to the boil. Pour in the oatmeal and again bring to boiling point. The gruel should then be simmered gently for 1/2 hour. Add the salt and sugar. A little cream makes the gruel smoother. To give colour and interest, a sliced fresh strawberry could be dotted on the surface.

Sailor's gruel was known as loblolly. The surgeon's assistant at sea was known as the Loblolly boy.

Flowers, fruit and herbs used in cooking and drink making were gathered when the dew had dried off them and before the sun became too hot. Fruit should be just ripe. This cough remedy is very old, coming from a fragment of manuscript dated 1860.

In the famous Roman city of Bath we lodged in Pulteney Street and bought Sally Lunns. Celebrated for a host of other reasons, the gateway to Somerset mirrors long history; before the Romans came it was the half-legendary town founded by Bladud. Literary associations stem from Jane Austen, Oliver Goldsmith, Charles Dickens, Edmund Spenser, the diarist Pepys and many others. This photograph taken in 1928 shows the Roman bath of Aquae Sulis, 20 feet below modern street level, with the towers of Bath Abbey in the background.

Somerset Scones

2 lb flour	1 teaspoon salt
3 teaspoons baking powder	3 oz butter
3 oz cream	2 eggs

Sift flour and salt into a bowl and add baking powder. Rub in the butter until mixture resembles breadcrumbs and beat in the eggs with the cream. A little milk may also be necessary to produce a firm, clean dough. Knead well then roll out and cut into rounds. Bake in a hot oven for 15 minutes until golden brown. These plain scones were cut in half fresh from the oven, served with home-made jam and lots of clotted cream. Old recipes often have large quantities as families and farmhands had to be fed. Half quantities might suffice as scones need to be made in fresh batches frequently. Stale, they are not interesting.

Blackberry Vinegar

Midland and Northern regions tend to favour raspberry vinegar, but the West Country, so prolific in blackberries, used these as their sore throat remedy 100 years ago and more.

4 lb blackberries	juice produced
1 lb sugar to each pint of	2 pints vinegar

Wash and crush the blackberries, then pour 2 pints of vinegar over, or enough to cover. Leave them covered for a whole day then boil with the sugar for 25 minutes. It should thicken a little. Bottle when cold. A tablespoonful in a glass of hot water makes a delicious drink, quite apart from colds.

Plum Sauce

can also be served with roast lamb

1 lb golden plums	1/2 pint wine vinegar
1 tablespoon chopped fresh mint	4 oz sugar
	2 tablespoons water

Stone and wash the fruit and place in a saucepan with the sugar. Simmer gently with the water until the plums are soft. Add the vinegar and bring to the boil. Cook on until the plums thicken. Beat well, stirring in the fresh chopped mint. Serve warm with the roast lamb.

An old Somerset custom is called "Bringing in the bread and cheese". A huge loaf and a huge cheese are borne in on the shoulders of farmworkers.

Somerset Herb Cheese

1/2 lb Cheddar cheese	2 tablespoons chopped chives
6 tablespoons cream	and parsley

Grate the cheese and with the other ingredients render it down in a double saucepan, stirring all the time for maximum creaminess. Pour into small pots and cool. The herbs make it a delicate green-blue in colour.

Honey Pudding

4oz breadcrumbs made crispy   4 oz flour
4 tablespoons runny honey   4 oz shredded suet
4 oz currants and raisins   1 teaspoon baking powder
a little milk

Mix all the ingredients together and mix them well into a stiff consistency. Place in a greased basin, allowing for some expansion. Cover with layers of pleated, buttered paper and steam for 2 1/2 hours.

Somerset honey was used widely in recipes for puddings, cakes and in the cooking of ham and chicken. We used Richard Bolton's honey of Mill Fruit Farm Stogumber and found it excellent in this recipe.

Cheese Pudding

Break 1 egg. Mix it with 2 tablespoons of milk, 1 of breadcrumbs, 1/4 lb of grated cheese. If the cheese is very dry add 1/2 oz of butter. Put in a mould and boil for 40 minutes or bake with breadcrumbs and a scatter of nutmeg.

Norton St. Philip is famed for this magnificent coaching inn, The George, which is claimed to be the oldest licensed house in England. Dating from the 15th. century, it features long, narrow passages, low ceilings, leaded window panes and hidden nooks, an inn that has greeted wayfarers and dispensed Somerset food prepared from old recipes for hundreds of years. This photograph was taken more than fifty years ago.

Rosemary Syrup

2 pints water   a handful of rosemary
sugar

Pour the boiling water onto the chopped rosemary and leave it to stand overnight. Strain the liquid next day and to each pint of liquid add 1 lb sugar. Boil until syrupy and allow to cool, when it may be bottled. A sore throat remedy.

Somerset lavender grows into huge bushes in places like Watchet, Minehead, Blue Anchor, Porlock, Old Cleeve and Wootton Courtenay. It was so prolific, bags and pillows could be stuffed with flowers which scented chests, wardrobes, drawers, presses, and went into pot pourri bowls.

Dandelion Wine

To make 2 gallons :

Pour 4 quarts of boiling water over 5 quarts of washed dandelion flowers and leave to stand. Next day boil 4 quarts of water with 8 lb of sugar and the rind of 1 lemon and 2 oranges. Strain the liquor off the flowers and place all together in a large crock. Mix 1 oz yeast with some of the warm (not hot) liquor, then add it to the whole in the crock. Put it into large stone jars and allow it to work for 3 weeks, filling up the jars with boiled water for the first 2 weeks. Cork and leave for 6 months, then put into small, sterilised bottles but do not disturb the sediment.

Old-Fashioned Vegetable Soup from Crowcombe

1 tablespoon oatmeal   1 cup chopped onion
1 cup chopped carrot   1/2 cup chopped celery
2 tablespoons butter   water

Brown the vegetables in the butter then place all in 3 pints of boiling water and cook for 45 minutes at a simmer. Add the oatmeal and boil again for another 10 minutes. Adjust seasoning.

Amongst the Rules of a Somerset Coffee House in 1674 was: "He that shall any quarrel here begin, shall give each man a dish to atone the sin." Carwardines, Coffee Roasters and Blenders since 1777, from early days sold "the finest souchong tea". Their Bristol coffee house was opened at 56 Corn Street in the 1920s to complement the flourishing tea and coffee business. Dishes of this vegetable soup would atone nicely.

Hasty Pudding

3/4 pint warm milk   pinch grated nutmeg
2 oz sugar   2 oz butter
1 1/2 tablespoons flour

Melt half the butter in a saucepan and stir in the flour. Gradually add the warm milk, stirring all the time. You will feel the mixture thicken. Add the pinch of nutmeg and stir on till quite smooth. Pour the mixture into a buttered dish. Dot with rest of butter, sprinkle with sugar and place under the grill for a few minutes until the top is melted and brown. Hasty Pudding may well have been the poor man's burnt cream to go with his "Poor Man's Goose".

Mixed Herbs

From the herb gardens attached to country houses or cottages the following herbs were gathered and dried:

2 oz marjoram   1 oz thyme
1 oz lemon thyme   1 oz winter savory
1 oz basil   2 oz parsley
1/2 oz tarragon

This was the proportion. Rubbed down and mixed, they were kept in closely covered jars or crocks. The reference to "sweet herbs" in old recipes meant their use.

Egg Poached in Cream

1 egg   1 oz butter
2 tablespoons fresh cream   seasoning

Butter a small ramekin, put in the cream and break the egg carefully into it, sprinkling with salt and pepper. Stand the ramekin in a small pan containing water half way up the sides of the dish containing the egg. Simmer very gently until the egg is set. A little grated Cheddar cheese on top of the egg makes a change.

Hele Bridge, Dulverton, over the River Exe, is part of a market town and home of the Exmoor National Park Centre at Exmoor House. The town, which on some days is thronged with farmers, tourists, huntsmen and fishermen, used to have a Norman fort. "Abandon diet sheets, all ye who enter here", joked one tourist, who was thoroughly enjoying Somerset fare.

Hele Bridge. Dulverton.

SNOW ON TARR STEPS

VOWLES

Plum Syrup for Fruit Salads

7 lb plums   7 lb sugar
brandy

Boil the plums with sugar for 20 minutes. Pour through a sieve and drain. Measure the syrup and to each quart add 1 teaspoon of brandy. Bottle and cork well. The plum pulp can be made into:

Pickled Plums

which is good with Christmas meats

3 lb plums   1 teaspoon all spice
2 lb sugar   1 teaspoon ginger
4 pints vinegar   1 teaspoon ground cloves

Put the fruit or fruit pulp in with the sugar. Add the spices and vinegar and cook until tender. Drain well and put into jars. Boil the syrup for 1/4 hour and strain into the jars. On the next day put off the syrup, re-boil and pour over the fruit again. Allow to go cold, cover and store for 3 months. Pickled in September, the plums are ready for use on the Christmas dinner table.

Tarr Steps, the ancient clapper bridge, in snow is one of the loveliest sights of a Somerset unchanged, as are the many beautiful small villages with whitewashed cottages smothered in clematis. The primitive stone causeway was built unknown ages ago, one of the finest prehistoric monuments of its kind in England. The slabs average 7 ft. long in this 180 ft. bridge here photographed in the 1920s.

Stowey Apple Pudding

On Twelfth Night the farmers of Somerset wassailed their apple trees, a pagan custom, standing around in a circle and singing to encourage a good apple crop for puddings, pies, cider and windfalls for the pigs.

1 lb apples
suet crust

Prepare the apples - wash, core, peel, chop and place in a pudding basin lined with crust and cover with a pastry lid. It was served with sweet cider sauce and it was unnecessary to add either sugar or water to the pudding.

Cucumber for the Complexion

Peel 2 large cucumbers and cut into thin slices. Place in a double saucepan, adding no water to the cucumber, and cook until soft. Place the pieces in muslin and squeeze out all the juice. Add to the juice an equal amount of elderflower water. Shake well. Seal in clean bottles. Used when skin was roughened by wind or sea air or for blemishes in the complexion.

Rabbit Mould

Cut up and stew a rabbit until it is tender in 3 pints of water, to which has been added 2 sliced, peeled onions, 3 large peeled, sliced carrots and a pinch of nutmeg. Remove the meat from the rabbit and press it into a wetted mould. To the stock in which the rabbit was boiled add 2 oz of gelatine. Bring to the boil then strain it over the meat in the mould. Place it on a marble slab to go completely cold and set. Serve with cucumber salad.

Somerset Farm Cider

1 peck windfall apples   demerara Sugar
1 gallon boiling water

Wash apples and cut up roughly. Pour the boiling water over them. Allow to stand for 2 weeks. Strain and add 1 lb demerara sugar to each quart of liquor.

On January 17th at Carhampton, Somerset, the custom of wassailing the apple trees is still part of the folklore calendar.

At Malmsmead the Badgworthy and Oare rivers meet to form the Lyn. The river flowing through the Doone Valley is a tributary of the Badgworthy which forms the boundary between Devon and Somerset. This photograph of Malmsmead Bridge and Lorna Doone Farm dates from the 1900s. Exmoor, the land of wild red deer and the soaring buzzard, is the area now famous for scones, splits, jam and clotted cream, served at similar farmhouses, but Lorna remains famous, inspiring such delightful confectionery as Lorna's Cream Slices.

Dandelion and Ginger Wine

End of April and into May is the time to make this lovely brew. All the way from Somerset to Devon golden, glowing dandelions smiled down the winding lanes and across the fields.

1 gallon of dandelion heads   1 gallon boiling water
1 lemon   1 oz ground ginger
8 oz raisins   1 orange
5 lb sugar   yeast
1/2 pint cold tea

The flowers should be covered with the boiling water, left for 3 days and stirred frequently. The liquid should then be strained and the ginger, orange and lemon rinds added. Bring to the boil and simmer the solution for 35 minutes.

Now squeeze the juices from the lemon and orange and add immediately to the raisins and sugar in another container. Upon this should be strained the cool liquid. Add the tea and sprinkle about 2 oz yeast on top. Cover and leave in a warm place to ferment for 8 days. Strain the wine into a one gallon jar. As the wine clears it can be bottled. Keep till Christmas.

Dunkery Lemonade

the rind of 4 lemons cut fine   the juice of 6 lemons
4 lb sugar   1 oz tartaric acid
1 oz citric acid   3 pints water

Mix together and pour on the 3 pints of water, boiling. In use it will dilute.

Acknowledgements

I should like to thank
Margaret Ames
Major John Andrews
Erica Bloss
Mary Bowden
Nicola Bunn
Stanley Butterworth
Carwardines, Bristol
Alan Chidgey
Miss M. Don
Kathleen George
Natalie Green
Halsway Manor, Crowcombe
Jill Hancock Toys
Lillian Harrod
Andrea Hewer
Dawn Heywood
Max Ley
Del Lister
Louise Macarthy
Magpie Antiques

Sue Marshall
The National Trust
W.H. "Ben" Norman
Nicola Puddy
Ron Severs
The Shaul Bakery
Thelma Snape
Somerset County Council Library Service
Somerset Record Office
Sarah Sparks
June Thomas
Tourist Information Centres: Bath, Bridgwater, Glastonbury, Minehead
Ken Viggars
West Somerset Rural Life Museum
Richard Wheeler
The White Lion, Bridgwater
Ye Olde Willow Tea Rooms, Cannington
Julie Young
and the many other kind people, whose names in the hurly burly of note-taking we failed to record.